D0926742

Life Under the Sea

Seals

by Cari Meister

Bullfrog
Books

Ideas for Parents and Teachers

Bullfrog Books give children practice reading nonfiction at the earliest levels. Repetition, familiar words, and photos support early readers.

Before Reading

- Discuss the cover photo with the class. What does it tell them?
- Look at the picture glossary together. Read and discuss the words.

Read the Book

- "Walk" through the book and look at the photos. Let the child ask questions.
- Read the book to the child, or have him or her read independently.

After Reading

- Prompt the child to think more. Ask: What kinds of sea animals do you think eat seals?

Bullfrog Books are published by Jump!
5357 Penn Avenue South
Minneapolis, MN 55419
www.jumplibrary.com

Library of Congress Cataloging-in-Publication Data
Meister, Cari.
 Seals / by Cari Meister.
  p. cm. -- (Bullfrog books: life under the sea)
 Summary: "This photo-illustrated nonfiction story for young readers describes the body parts of seals and how they hunt for food under the sea. Includes picture glossary"--Provided by publisher.
 Includes bibliographical references and index.
 ISBN 978-1-62031-011-3 (hbk. : alk. paper)
 1. Seals (Animals)--Juvenile literature. I. Title.
 QL737.P64M44 2013
 599.79--dc23
                                                        2012008433

Series Editor: Rebecca Glaser
Series Designer: Ellen Huber
Production: Chelsey Luther

Photo Credits: Dreamstime, 1, 6, 24; Getty, 6-7, 15, 23tr; National Geographic Stock, 16-17, 18-19; Shutterstock, 12-13, 14t, 14b, 18, 23br, 23tl; SuperStock, cover, 5, 8-9, 10, 11, 20-21, 23bl; Veer, 3t, 3b, 4, 22

Printed in the United States of America at Corporate Graphics in North Mankato, Minnesota
7-2012/ PO 1125
10 9 8 7 6 5 4 3 2 1

Table of Contents

Seals Under the Sea

A seal is hungry.
How does she
find food?

Seals like to
be on land.

But they love
to hunt in
the water.

Seals are fast
swimmers.

Their long bodies
help them glide.

fore
flipper

Seals have flippers.
Fore flippers help
seals steer.

Hind flippers help seals go fast.

Seals have big eyes.

They can see under water.

Watch out squid!
Watch out fish!

Watch out crab!

14

**A seal is coming!
She may eat you!**

Seals dive deep.

They hold their breath.

whisker

Seals have whiskers
on their snouts.
Whiskers feel the ocean floor.

The seal finds a fish.

Yum!

Parts of a Seal

whiskers
Stiff hairs around the seal's mouth that help sense things.

snout
The part of a seal's head that sticks out; the snout includes the nose and mouth.

fore flippers
The front, flat limbs of a seal that help a seal steer while swimming.

hind flippers
The back, flat limbs of a seal that help a seal swim forward.

Picture Glossary

crab
An ocean animal with eight legs, a hard shell, and two claws.

hunt
To look for food.

dive
To go head first under water.

squid
An ocean animal with a long soft body, eight arms, and two tentacles.

Index

To Learn More

Learning more is as easy as 1, 2, 3.

1) Go to www.factsurfer.com

2) Enter "seal" into the search box.

3) Click the "Surf" button to see a list of websites.

With factsurfer.com, finding more information is just a click away.